PLATO'S EUTHYPHRO, APOLOGY, AND CRITO

Arranged for Dramatic Presentation from the Jowett translation with Choruses

S.W. Emery

University Press of America, Inc.
Lanham • New York • London

Copyright © 1996 by
S. W. Emery
University Press of America,® Inc.
4720 Boston Way
Lanham, Maryland 20706

3 Henrietta Street
London, WC2E 8LU England

Library of Congress Cataloging-in-Publication Data

Emery, Sarah Watson
Plato's Euthyphro, Apology, and Crito : arranged for dramatic
presentation from the Jowett translation with choruses / S. W. Emery.
p.   cm.
1. Socrates--Drama. 2. Philosophers--Greece--Drama. 3.
Philosophy, Ancient--Drama. 4. Plato-Adaptations.   I. Plato.
Euthyphro. I. Plato. Apology. III. Plato. Crito. IV. Title.
PS3555.M427P58   1995   812' .54 --dc20   95-44385 CIP

ISBN 0-7618-0170-7 (cloth: alk: ppr.)

⊖™The paper used in this publication meets the minimum
requirements of American National Standard for information
Sciences—Permanence of Paper for Printed Library Materials,
ANSI Z39.48—1984

In memory of

Stephen Albert Emery 1902-1991

Contents

Foreword

When someone says that he wishes to engage in "meaningful dialogue," he means, at the very least, that he wants the conversation to have something personal and dramatic about it. The man who wants "meaningful dialogue" wants to overcome the impersonality and remoteness and abstraction of much contemporary life. His trouble is that he thinks he can do so without a genuine dramatic situation; he thinks that simply by appealing to you sincerely for sincerity he can attain what he wants. But real, and true, dramatic situations must grow up naturally. Our lives which are generally so plotless and diffuse, with loose ends and unfinished chapters, do not often provide us with such real, or true, dramatic situations. It is for this reason that we turn to art--to television dramas, to movies, to novels, or, if we have any sense, to the great works of tragedy and of Plato. For Plato, who started out, we are told, to be a tragedian, is unique among philosophers. He alone of all philosophers understood that truth, even the most abstract truth, must start from a dramatic situation. That is the reason that he wrote dialogues. Well, then, true philosophy must take its origin from an authentic dramatic situation. We know this truth from our own personal experience: personal crises drive us to philosophy. A friend betrays us, and we ask, "What is loyalty?" A beloved dies, and we ask, "What is death?" But because we wait until some personal crisis grieves us to begin philosophizing, we find that we must try to philosophize when we are at our worst, when we are stricken with grief, when our minds are clouded by resentment or hatred or fear. As usual the Greeks are there--or rather here--to help us, for it is they who discovered that art is the best way to confront crises. Great art is paradigmatic, by which I mean, it provides us with living dramatic paradigms and models and examples of the great crises of life, which we can live vicariously, by proxy, second-hand, and yet with a rich and full sense of dramatic immediacy and texture and tension. Such is the reason Plato wrote dialogues.

The more we can read Plato's dialogues as dramas, the more we can derive from them the sort of inspirational purpose they have been achieving for nearly two and a half millennia. Throughout this great expanse of human history Plato stirred many souls to philosophy, souls that would otherwise have passed their lives without self-examination, without the sensitive moral awareness that separates the intentionally good person from the one accidentally good, without the abiding trust in rational argument to arrive at wise decisions.

The dialogues Dr. Emery presents here in dramatic adaptation are among the most stirring Plato wrote. Plato's genius and the genius of his spiritual guide Socrates shine forth in all brilliant radiance. Let these characters now join the troupe of great *dramatis personae* on the stage of the world's plays; let them join Hamlet and Lear, let them join Oedipus and Antigone; let Plato's dream be fulfilled. And let the plays stir the souls of whole new generations.

James A. Arieti
Hampden-Sydney College

Preface

In presenting Plato's *Euthyphro*, *Apology*, and *Crito* in dramatic form, with choruses added to the text, I have sought to offer these related dialogues as a partial portrayal of the last days in the life of Socrates. The work is intended for both students and all others who are interested in our heritage from the ancient Greeks. The fact that we know so much about Socrates after over two millennia is a privilege and a blessing which I have tried to share with the reader or an audience, if the works are ever presented on stage.

My primary acknowledgment must go to the late Professor Albert Avey of the Department of Philosophy at Ohio State University, who first introduced me to Plato in the summer of 1937. I am also indebted to the many scholars who have translated or commented upon the dialogues of Plato. In particular, I wish to acknowledge my debt to Professor James A. Arieti for his book, *Interpreting Plato: The Dialogues as Drama*, which confirms the legitimacy of this effort to dramatize some of the dialogues of Plato. In addition, I am most grateful to Professor Arieti, Dean Eva T. H. Brann, Professor David E. Hahm, and Professor Ronald Polansky for kindly reading parts or all of the manuscript and commenting upon it, and especially to Professor Dorothy Jones for encouraging me throughout this enterprise. And, most of all, I am indebted to my late husband, Stephen Albert Emery, for not only encouraging my work, but also for personifying in his life and career the spirit of Socrates.

June 1995   S.W.E.

EUTHYPHRO

Cast of Characters

SOCRATES: A citizen of Athens, friend and teacher of Plato as well as Alcibiades, an Athenian who became a traitor to his city-state. Socrates was a stone-cutter by profession and had served Athens in an honorable military career. He is here portrayed on his way to his trial, where he is being charged by Meletus, a tool of the politician, Anytus, with impiety. A.E. Taylor in *Plato: the Man and His Work* says,

> We may fairly suppose that what he (Anytus) attributed to Socrates was the corruption of the young men; and that this meant exercising an influence hostile to the temper of unquestioning loyalty to the democracy.

Irwin Edman in *The Works of Plato* says of Socrates,

> If logic was the method, ethics was the central interest of Socrates, and it is this dominant concern with the good and the good life that seems most forcibly to have impressed Plato.

Socrates is seventy years old.

EUTHYPHRO: A respected citizen of Athens who is prosecuting his aged father on charges of an involuntary murder of a servant. As A.E. Taylor says, Euthyphro's "object...is to clear *himself* from the religious pollution incurred by being in any way accessory to a murder." Euthyphro is a young "know-it all."

CHORUS: Two or more Athenian citizens.

SCENE: Athens, at that time a city-state. The porch of the King Archon.

TIME: 399 B.C.

SETTING: The porch in front of the building where Socrates is to be tried. The porch extends the full width of the stage, with two columns, right and left, and an entry to the building at the rear. Across the front of the porch is an area of a few feet one step lower than the porch.

AT RISE: The CHORUS stands at LEFT in front of the Porch.

CHORUS

The time has come to give this strange, strange man
His due. Our sons were killed in war against
Sparta, or went with Xenophon to Persia.
Sparta has won with and without the aid
Of our own Alcibiades--
There must be someone to accuse and blame.
We've seen him wandering in the marketplace.
"Public enemy" he's called. We have
Been warned by Aristophanes and others.
The Sophist Socrates has looked into
The Unseen below the earth and in the Heavens,
Replacing gods which we have long revered.
Evil and chaos dwell with us today.
Young men follow him; Alcibiades,
The noble one, has been corrupted.
There sit at his feet Plato and his brother.
In trial we will judge this Socrates
For bringing in a new god of his own,
A god of reason we have never known.

(ENTER EUTHYPHRO at Left. A few seconds later ENTER SOCRATES from Right. Each steps up the step to the porch as he speaks)

EUTHYPHRO
Why have you left the Lyceum, Socrates? and what are you doing in the porch of the King Archon? Surely you cannot be concerned in a suit before the king, like myself?

SOCRATES
Not in a suit, Euthyphro; impeachment is the word which the Athenians use.

EUTHYPHRO
What! I suppose that someone has been prosecuting you, for I cannot believe that you are the prosecutor of another.

SOCRATES
Certainly not.

EUTHYPHRO
Then someone else has been prosecuting you?

SOCRATES
Yes.

EUTHYPHRO
And who is he?

SOCRATES
A young man who is little known. I hardly know him; his name is Meletus. Perhaps you may remember his

appearance; he has a beak, and long straight hair, and a beard which is ill grown.

EUTHYPHRO

No, I do not remember him. But what is the charge which he brings against you?

SOCRATES

What is the charge? Well, a very serious charge, which shows a good deal of character in the young man. He says he knows how the youth are corrupted and who are their corrupters. I fancy that he must be a wise man, and seeing that I am the reverse of a wise man, he has found me out, and is going to accuse me of corrupting his young friends. And of this our mother the State is to be the judge. Of all our political men he is the only one who seems to begin in the right way, with the cultivation of virtue in youth; and if he goes on as he has begun, he will be a very great public benefactor.

EUTHYPHRO

I hope that he may; but I rather fear, Socrates, that the opposite will turn out to be the truth. In what way does he say that you corrupt the young?

SOCRATES

He brings a wonderful accusation against me. He says that I am a poet or maker of gods, and that I invent new gods and deny the existence of old ones; this is the ground of his indictment.

EUTHYPHRO

I understand, Socrates; he means to attack you about the familiar sign which occasionally, as you say, comes to you, and he is going to have you up before the court for this. He knows that such a charge is readily received by the world, as I myself know too well; for when I speak in the assembly about divine things, and foretell the future to them, they laugh at me and think me a madman. But they are jealous of us all; and we must be brave and go at them.

SOCRATES
Their laughter, friend Euthyphro, is not a matter of much consequence. For a man may be thought wise; but the Athenians do not much trouble themselves about him until he begins to impart his wisdom to others, and then for some reason or other, perhaps, as you say, from jealousy, they are angry.

EUTHYPHRO
I am never likely to try their temper in this way.

SOCRATES
I dare say not, for you seldom impart your wisdom. But I have a benevolent habit of pouring out myself to everybody, and would even pay for a listener. What the end will be you soothsayers only can predict.

EUTHYPHRO
I dare say that the affair will end in nothing, Socrates, and that you will win your cause; and I think that I shall win my own.

SOCRATES
And what is your suit, Euthyphro? are you the pursuer or the defendant?

EUTHYPHRO

I am the pursuer.

SOCRATES

Of whom?

EUTHYPHRO

You will think me mad when I tell you.

SOCRATES

Why, has the fugitive wings?

EUTHYPHRO

Nay, he is not very volatile at his time of life.

SOCRATES

Who is he?

EUTHYPHRO

My father.

SOCRATES

Your father! My good man?

EUTHYPHRO

Yes.

SOCRATES

And of what is he accused?

EUTHYPHRO

Of murder, Socrates.

SOCRATES

By the powers, Euthyphro! I suppose that the man whom your father murdered was one of your relatives--for if he had been a stranger you would never have thought of prosecuting him.

EUTHYPHRO

I am amused, Socrates, at your making a distinction between one who is a relation and one who is not a relation. The real question is whether the murdered man has been justly slain. Now, the man who is dead worked for us as a field laborer on our farm in Naxos, and one day in a fit of drunken passion he got into a quarrel with one of our domestic servants and slew him. My father bound him hand and foot and threw him into a ditch, and then sent to Athens to ask of a diviner what he should do with him. Meanwhile he never attended to him, for he regarded him as a murderer, and thought that no great harm would be done even if he did die. Now this was just what happened. For such was the effect of cold and hunger and chains upon him, that before the messenger returned from the diviner, he was dead. And my father and family are angry with me for taking the part of the murderer, and prosecuting my father. They say that he did not kill him, and that if he did, the dead man was but a murderer, and I ought not to take any notice, for that a son is impious who prosecutes a father. Which shows, Socrates, how little they know what the gods think about piety and impiety.

SOCRATES

Good heavens, Euthyphro! and is your knowledge of religion and of things pious and impious so very exact, that, supposing the circumstances to be as you state them, you are not afraid lest you too may be doing an impious thing in bringing an action against your father?

EUTHYPHRO

The best of Euthyphro, and that which distinguishes him from other men, is his exact knowledge of all such matters. What should I be good for without it?

SOCRATES

Rare friend! I think that I cannot do better than be your disciple. Therefore, Euthyphro, I beg you to tell me the nature of piety and impiety, and of murder, and of other offenses against the gods. What are they? Is not piety in every action always the same? and impiety, again--is it not always the opposite of piety?

EUTHYPHRO

To be sure, Socrates.

SOCRATES

And what is piety, and what is impiety?

EUTHYPHRO

Piety is doing as I am doing; that is to say, prosecuting anyone who is guilty of murder, sacrilege, or of any similar crime--whether he be your father or mother, or whoever he may be--that makes no difference; and not to prosecute them is impiety. For do not men regard Zeus as the best and most righteous of the gods?--and yet they admit that he bound his father, Cronos, because he wickedly devoured his sons, and that he too had punished his own father, Uranus, for a similar reason, in a nameless manner. And yet when I proceed against my father, they are angry with me. So inconsistent are they.

SOCRATES

May not this be the reason, Euthyphro, why I am charged with impiety--that I cannot believe these stories about the gods? Tell me, whether you really believe that they are true.

EUTHYPHRO

Yes, Socrates; and things more wonderful still, of which the world is in ignorance.

SOCRATES

And do you really believe that the gods fought with one another, as the poets say, and as you may see represented in the works of great artists? Are these tales of the gods true, Euthyphro?

EUTHYPHRO

Yes, Socrates; and I can tell you many other things about the gods which would quite amaze you.

SOCRATES

I dare say. But at present I would rather hear from you a more precise answer, which you have not as yet given to the question, What is "piety"? When asked, you only replied, Doing as you do, charging your father with murder.

EUTHYPHRO

And what I said is true, Socrates.

SOCRATES

No doubt, Euthyphro; but you would admit that there are many other pious acts?

EUTHYPHRO

There are.

SOCRATES

Remember that I did not ask you to give me two or three examples of piety, but to explain the general idea which makes all pious things to be pious. Do you not recollect that there was one idea which made the impious impious, and the pious pious?

EUTHYPHRO

I remember.

SOCRATES

Tell me what is the nature of this idea, and then I shall be able to say that such and such an action is pious, such another impious.

EUTHYPHRO

I will tell you, if you like.

SOCRATES

I should very much like.

EUTHYPHRO

Piety, then, is that which is dear to the gods, and impiety is that which is not dear to them.

SOCRATES

Very good, Euthyphro; you have now given me the sort of answer which I wanted. Come, then, and let us examine it. That thing or person which is dear to the gods is pious, and that thing or person which is hateful to the gods is impious, these two being the extreme opposites of one another. Was not that said?

EUTHYPHRO

It was.

SOCRATES

And further, Euthyphro, the gods were admitted to have enmities and hatreds and differences?

EUTHYPHRO

Yes, that was also said.

SOCRATES

And what sort of difference creates enmity and anger? I dare say the answer does not occur to you at the moment, and therefore I will suggest that these enmities arise when the matters of difference are the just and unjust, good and evil, honourable and dishonourable. Are not these the points about which men differ, and about which when we are unable satisfactorily to decide our differences, you and I and all of us quarrel, when we do quarrel?

EUTHYPHRO

Yes, Socrates, the nature of the differences about which we quarrel is such as you describe.

SOCRATES

And the quarrels of the gods, noble Euthyphro, when they occur, are of a like nature?

EUTHYPHRO

Certainly they are.

SOCRATES

They have differences of opinion, as you say, about good and evil, just and unjust, honourable and dishonourable: there would have been no quarrels among them, if there had been no such differences--would there now?

EUTHYPHRO

You are quite right.

SOCRATES

Then the same things are hated by the gods and loved by the gods, and are both hateful and dear to them?

EUTHYPHRO

True.

SOCRATES

And upon this view the same things, Euthyphro, will be pious and also impious?

EUTHYPHRO

So I should suppose.

SOCRATES

Then, my friend, I remark with surprise that you have not answered the question which I asked. It would seem that what is loved by the gods is also hated by them. And therefore, Euthyphro, in thus chastising your father you may very likely be doing what is agreeable to Zeus but disagreeable to Cronos or Uranus, and there may be other gods who have similar differences of opinion.

EUTHYPHRO

But I believe, Socrates, that all the gods would be agreed as to the propriety of punishing a murderer: there would be no difference of opinion about that.

SOCRATES

Well, but speaking of men, Euthyphro, did you ever hear anyone arguing that a murderer or any sort of evildoer ought to be let off? My dear friend, do tell me, for my better instruction and information, how would you show that all the gods absolutely agree in approving the act of a son proceeding against his father and accusing him of murder in such a case as yours? Prove to me that they do, and I will applaud your wisdom as long as I live.

EUTHYPHRO

It will be a difficult task; but I could make the matter very clear indeed to you.

SOCRATES

There was a notion that came into my mind while you were speaking. I said to myself: "Well, and what if Euthyphro does prove to me that all the gods regarded the death of the serf as unjust, how do I know anything more of the nature of piety and impiety?" Therefore, Euthyphro, I do not ask you to prove this; I will suppose, if you like, that all the gods condemn and abominate such an action. But I will amend the definitions so far as to say that what all the gods hate is impious, and what they love pious or holy; and what some of them love and others hate is both or neither. Shall this be our definition of piety and impiety?

EUTHYPHRO
Yes, I should say that what all the gods love is pious and holy, and the opposite which they all hate, impious.

SOCRATES
The point which I should first wish to understand is whether the pious or holy is beloved by the gods because it is holy, or holy because it is beloved of the gods.

EUTHYPHRO
I do not understand your meaning, Socrates.

SOCRATES
What do you say of piety, Euthyphro: is not piety, according to your definition, loved by all the gods?

EUTHYPHRO
Yes.

SOCRATES
Because it is pious or holy, or for some other reason?

EUTHYPHRO
No, that is the reason.

SOCRATES
It is loved because it is holy, not holy because it is loved?

EUTHYPHRO
Yes.

SOCRATES
You appear to me, Euthyphro, when I ask you what is the essence of holiness, to offer an attribute only, and not the

essence--the attribute of being loved by all the gods. But you still refuse to explain to me the nature of holiness. And therefore, if you please, I will ask you not to hide your treasure, but to tell me once more what holiness or piety really is, whether dear to the gods or not (for that is a matter about which we will not quarrel); and what is impiety?

EUTHYPHRO
I really do not know, Socrates, how to express what I mean. For somehow or other our arguments, on whatever ground we rest them, seem to turn round and walk away from us.

SOCRATES
Tell me, then,--Is not that which is pious necessarily just?

EUTHYPHRO
Yes.

SOCRATES
And is, then, all which is just pious? or, is that which is pious all just, but that which is just, only in part and not all, pious?

EUTHYPHRO
I do not understand you, Socrates.

SOCRATES
And yet I know that you are as much wiser than I am, as you are younger. But, revered friend, the abundance of your wisdom makes you lazy. The odd is a part of the number, and number is a more extended notion than the odd. I suppose that you follow me now?

EUTHYPHRO
Quite well.

SOCRATES
That was the sort of question which I meant to raise when I asked whether justice is the more extended notion of which piety is only a part. Do you dissent?

EUTHYPHRO
No, I think that you are quite right.

SOCRATES
Then, if piety is a part of justice, I suppose that we should inquire what part? I want you to tell me what part of justice is piety or holiness, that I may be able to tell Meletus not to do me injustice, or indict me for impiety, as I am now adequately instructed by you in the nature of piety or holiness, and their opposites.

EUTHYPHRO
Piety or holiness, Socrates, appears to me to be that part of justice which attends to the gods, as there is the other part of justice which attends to men.

SOCRATES
That is good, Euthyphro; yet still there is a little point about which I should like to have further information. What is the meaning of "attention"? For instance, horses are said to require attention, and not every person is able to attend to them, but only a person skilled in horsemanship. Is it not so?

EUTHYPHRO
Certainly.

SOCRATES

I should suppose that the art of horsemanship is the art of attending to horses?

EUTHYPHRO

Yes.

SOCRATES

In like manner holiness or piety is the art of attending to the gods?--that would be your meaning, Euthyphro?

EUTHYPHRO

Yes.

SOCRATES

And is not attention always designed for the good or benefit of that to which the attention is given?

EUTHYPHRO

True.

SOCRATES

And does piety or holiness, which has been defined to be the art of attending to the gods, benefit or improve them? Would you say that when you do a holy act you make any of the gods better?

EUTHYPHRO

No, no; that was certainly not what I meant.

SOCRATES

And I, Euthyphro, never supposed that you did. I asked you the question about the nature of the attention, because I thought that you did not.

EUTHYPHRO

You do me justice, Socrates; that is not the sort of attention which I mean.

SOCRATES

Good: but I must still ask what is this attention to the gods which is called piety?

EUTHYPHRO

It is such, Socrates, as servants show to their masters.

SOCRATES

I understand--a sort of ministration to the gods.

EUTHYPHRO

Exactly.

SOCRATES

And now tell me, my good friend, about the art which ministers to the gods. For you must surely know if, as you say, you are of all men living the one who is best instructed in religion.

EUTHYPHRO

And I speak the truth, Socrates.

SOCRATES

Tell me, then, oh, tell me--what is that fair work which the gods do by the help of our ministrations?

EUTHYPHRO

Many and fair, Socrates, are the works which they do.

SOCRATES

And of the many and fair things done by the gods, which is the chief or principal one?

EUTHYPHRO

I have told you already, Socrates, that to learn all these things accurately will be very tiresome. Let me simply say that piety or holiness is learning how to please the gods in word and deed, by prayers and sacrifices.

SOCRATES

Now, I can only ask again, what is the pious, and what is piety? Do you mean that they are a sort of science of praying and sacrificing?

EUTHYPHRO

Yes, I do.

SOCRATES

And sacrificing is giving to the gods, and prayer is asking of the gods?

EUTHYPHRO

Yes, Socrates.

SOCRATES

Upon this view, then, piety is a science of asking and giving?

EUTHYPHRO

You understand me capitally, Socrates.

SOCRATES

Yes, my friend. Please then to tell me what is the nature of this service to the gods? Do you mean that we prefer requests and give gifts to them?

EUTHYPHRO

Yes, I do.

SOCRATES

Is not the right way of asking to ask of them what we want?

EUTHYPHRO

Certainly.

SOCRATES

And the right way of giving is to give to them in return what they want of us.

EUTHYPHRO

Very true, Socrates.

SOCRATES

Then piety, Euthyphro, is an art which gods and men have of doing business with one another?

EUTHYPHRO

That is an expression you may use, if you like.

SOCRATES

But I have no particular liking for anything but the truth. I wish, however, that you would tell me what benefit accrues to the gods from our gifts. If they give everything and we give nothing, that must be an affair of the business in which we have very greatly the advantage of them.

EUTHYPHRO

And do you imagine, Socrates, that any benefit accrues to the gods from our gifts?

SOCRATES

But if not, Euthyphro, what is the meaning of gifts which are conferred by us upon the gods?

EUTHYPHRO

What else, but tributes of honour; and, as I was just now saying, what pleases them?

SOCRATES

Piety, then, is pleasing to the gods, but not beneficial or dear to them.

EUTHYPHRO

I should say that nothing could be dearer.

SOCRATES

Then once more the assertion is repeated that piety is dear to the gods?

EUTHYPHRO

Certainly.

SOCRATES

And when you say this, can you wonder at your words not standing firm, but walking away? For the argument, as you will perceive, comes round to the same point. Were we not saying that the holy or pious was not the same with that which is loved of the gods?   Have you forgotten?

EUTHYPHRO
I quite remember.

SOCRATES
And are you not saying that what is loved of the gods is holy; and is not this the same as what is dear to them--do you see?

EUTHYPHRO
True.

SOCRATES
Then either we were wrong in our former assertion; or, if we were right then, we are wrong now.

EUTHYPHRO
One of the two must be true.

SOCRATES
Then we must begin again and ask, What is piety?   That is an enquiry which I shall never be weary of pursuing as far as in me lies.   For, if any man knows, you are he; and therefore I must detain you, like Proteus, until you tell. If you had not certainly known the nature of piety and impiety, I am confident that you would never, on behalf of a serf, have charged your aged father with murder.   I am sure, therefore, that you know the nature of piety and impiety.   Speak out then, my dear Euthyphro, and do not hide your knowledge.

EUTHYPHRO

Another time, Socrates; for I am in a hurry, and must go now.

(EXIT EUTHYPHRO hurriedly at Left along the porch)

SOCRATES

Alas! my companion, and will you leave me in despair? I was hoping that you would instruct me in the nature of piety and impiety; and then I might have cleared myself of Meletus and his indictment. I would have told him that I had been enlightened by Euthyphro, and had given up rash innovations and speculations, in which I indulged only through ignorance, and that now I am about to lead a better life.

(EXIT SOCRATES slowly at Right along the porch)

CHORUS

Now you see his ways. As he proceeds
To his own trial Socrates stops one
To ask what is this thing called piety.
A good and pious man is Euthyphro,
But Socrates takes none of his replies.
He badgers him with questions and objections.
Who cares indeed if pious or the holy
Is beloved by the gods because it is holy,
Or that the holy is holy because
It is beloved by them?
Where can we look if not here from the people
For justice for a fellow of this sort?
Five hundred citizens sit upon the case--
Our friends, the artisans, the merchants.
Meletus, the poet, brings the charges.
Justice will reign today for Socrates;

Let him talk on and on as he desires.
We are on guard against his eloquence--
This day the people judge.

CURTAIN

APOLOGY

Cast of Characters

SOCRATES: A citizen of Athens, 70 years old, on trial. In *Plato's Apology of Socrates and Crito* (1908), edited by Louis Dyer, T.D. Seymour says in the "Introduction":

> The formal terms of the indictment submitted by Meletus to the Archon Basileus...were: 'Socrates is guilty of not believing in the gods believed in by the state, and of introducing other new divinities. Moreover, he is guilty of corrupting the youth. The penalty proposed is death.'

In the play, *Clouds* (423 B.C.), Aristophanes humorously portrayed Socrates as worshipping the clouds and space. In truth, although Socrates was a master of the dialectic method, he was also a religious mystic, at times going into a trance and claiming also to hear a "Voice" speaking to him. It is not strange that, as he wandered about Athens questioning persons of all callings, a group of young men followed him to listen. Some of them became his disciples, while others, like the politicians, Alcibiades and Critias and Charmides, admirers and friends.

ANYTUS: According to A. E. Taylor in *Plato: the Man and His Work*, "one of the two most admired and trusted leaders of the restored democracy" in Athens. Democracy was restored in Athens in 403 B.C. when the Rule of the Thirty (404-403 B.C.) was overthrown and Critias, one of the leaders, was killed.   Anytus, although responsible for bringing Socrates to trial, did not take an active part in the trial. A. E. Taylor says,

> There was a reason why Anytus, could neither put his real case forward without disguise of some kind nor appear as the actual prosecutor...The worst 'offenses' of Socrates had been committed under the old democracy and all open reference to them was banned by the Act of Oblivion forbidding all questioning of citizens for anything done before the archonship of Euclides.

Socrates' chief offence in the old democracy was his refusal to participate in the trial of the Arginusae generals as a group. He had insisted that they be tried individually, according to the law. This was in 406 B.C.

LYCON: An obscure rhetorician of Athens, one of the accusers of Socrates, along with Anytus and Meletus.

MELETUS: A young tragic poet of Athens who was chosen by Anytus to conduct the prosecution of Socrates at the trial. According to A. E. Taylor, Meletus was

> a hopelessly crazy fanatic--the very man to make the right sort of tool for a political intrigue just because he combines absolute honesty with the simplicity of a half-wit.

BASILEUS: The King-Archon of Athens who presided at the trial.

MAGISTRATES: Two Magistrates seated on each side of Basileus.

PLATO: A young Athenian and friend of Socrates.

CRITO: A wealthy Athenian friend of the same age as Socrates.

CRITOBULUS: Son of Crito and a friend of Socrates.

APOLLODORUS: Young friend of Socrates.

JAILER: Athenian jailer.

JURORS: There were 500 jurors. The jurors were also the judges. The audience acts as the jurors, among whom are interspersed actors to demonstrate during the trial. The demonstrators are provided with cue cards bearing the words to be shouted.

CHORUS: Two or more Athenian citizens.

SCENE: The Court Room in Athens.

TIME: 399 B.C.

ACT I

Scene I

SETTING: The Court Room in Athens.

AT RISE: BASILEUS sits back center behind a low white stone table. On each side of him sits a MAGISTRATE. SOCRATES stands at LEFT, addressing the JURY, which is the audience. His friends, PLATO, CRITO, CRITOBULUS, and APOLLODORUS, sit at LEFT behind SOCRATES. His accusers, MELETUS, ANYTUS, and LYCON sit at RIGHT. ACTORS are interspersed among the audience to demonstrate during the Trial. The CHORUS stands at far LEFT.

CHORUS

It was a merry joke, we thought, when long
Since Socrates professed his creed to us
In the play of Aristophanes.
"Wide space," he said, "is what I hold exists
And there are clouds above me in the sky
As anyone can see, while to your ears
I speak with my most gifted tongue."
Thus you have seen the man and his crass tenets;
Strange gods he worships--clouds and space.
These things he taught to his disciples,
To Alcibiades and Critias,

And others he corrupted in their youth.
He once defied the old democracy
When ordered seven years ago to try
The generals for their thoughtless folly
After the Battle of Arginusae. On that day
He did not choose to do the people's will.
This day the people's will will reign again--
Democracy he disobeyed and spurned.
Alcibiades and Critias
Are not here now to help him. Let us see
Him stand before us. Let us listen to
The eloquence of which he boasts.

SOCRATES

How you, O Athenians, have been affected by my accusers, I cannot tell; but I know that they almost made me forget who I was--so persuasively did they speak; and yet they have hardly uttered a word of truth. But of the many falsehoods told by them, there was one which quite amazed me;--I mean when they said that you should be upon your guard and not allow yourselves to be deceived by the force of my eloquence. To say this, when they were certain to be detected as soon as I opened my lips and proved myself to be anything but a great speaker, did indeed appear to me most shameless --unless by the force of eloquence they mean the force of truth. From me you shall hear the whole truth.

At my time of life I ought not to be appearing before you, O men of Athens, in the character of a juvenile orator--let no one expect it of me. For I am more than seventy years of age, and appearing now for the first time in a court of law.

And first, I have to reply to the older charges and to my first accusers, and then I will go on to the later ones. For of old I have had many accusers, who have accused me falsely to you during many years; and I am more afraid of them than of Anytus and his associates, who are dangerous, too, in their own way. But far more dangerous are the others, who began when you were children, and took possession of your minds with their falsehoods, telling of one Socrates, a wise man, who speculated about the heaven above, and searched into the earth beneath, and made the worse appear the better cause. The disseminators of this tale are the accusers whom I dread.

I will ask you then to assume with me that my opponents are of two kinds; one recent, the other ancient: and I hope that you will see the propriety of my answering the latter first, for these accusations you heard long before the others, and much oftener. And so leaving the event with God, in obedience to the law I will now make my defence.

I will begin at the beginning, and ask what is the accusation which has given rise to the slander of me, and in fact has encouraged Meletus to prefer this charge against me. What do the slanderers say? I will sum up their words in an affidavit: "Socrates is an evildoer, and a curious person, who searches into things under the earth and in heaven, and he makes the worse appear the better cause; and he teaches the aforesaid doctrines to others." Such is the nature of the accusation: it is just what you have yourselves seen in the comedy of Aristophanes, who has introduced a man whom he calls Socrates, going about and saying that he walks in air, and talking a deal of nonsense concerning matters of which I do not pretend to know either much or little--not that I mean to speak disparagingly of any one who is a student of natural philosophy. But the simple truth is, O Athenians, that I have nothing to do with physical speculations. Very many of those here present are witnesses to the truth of this, and to them I appeal. Speak then, you who have heard me, and tell your neighbors whether any of you have ever known me hold forth in few words or in many upon such matters.

VOICES
(From the audience)

That's right, Socrates....You've never been a natural philosopher.... Aristophanes slandered you....That's right.

SOCRATES

You hear their answer. And from what they say of this part of the charge you will be able to judge of the truth of the rest.

As little foundation is there for the report that I am a teacher, and take money; this accusation has no more truth in it than the other.

I dare say, Athenians, that some one among you will reply, "Yes, Socrates, but what is the origin of these accusations which are brought against you; there must have been something strange which you have been doing? All these rumours and this talk about you would never have arisen if you had been like other men: tell us, then, what is the cause of them, for we would be sorry to judge hastily of you." Now, I regard this as a fair challenge, and I will endeavour to explain to you the reason why I am called wise and have such an evil fame. Please to attend then, Men of Athens, this reputation of mine has come of a certain sort of wisdom which I possess.

VOICES
(From the audience)
Ho, ho! Listen to the old fool....Ho, ho! he's a fool.

SOCRATES
And here, O men of Athens, I must beg you not to interrupt me, even if I seem to say something extravagant. For the word which I will speak is not mine. I will refer you to a witness who is worthy of credit; that witness shall be the god of Delphi. You must have known Chaerephon; he was early a friend of mine, and also a friend of yours. Well, Chaerephon, as you know, was very impetuous in all his doings, and he went to Delphi and boldly asked the oracle to tell him whether--

VOICES
(From the audience)
Shut up!...Boo-oo-oo!...We've heard enough...That's enough!...Boo-oo-oo!

SOCRATES
As I was saying, I must beg you not to interrupt. He asked the oracle to tell him whether any one was wiser than I was, and the Pythian prophetess answered, that there was no man wiser. Chaerephon is dead himself; but his brother, who is in court, will confirm the truth of what I am saying.

When I heard the answer, I said to myself, what can the god mean? And what is the interpretation of his riddle? For I know that I have no wisdom, small or great. After long consideration, I thought of a method of trying the question. I reflected that if I could only find a man wiser than myself, then I might go to the god with a refutation in my hand. I should say to him, "Here is a man who is wiser than I am; but you said that I was the wisest." Accordingly I went to one who had the reputation of wisdom, and observed him--his name I need not mention; he was a politician whom I selected for examination--and the result was as follows: When I began to talk with him, I could not help thinking that he was not really wise, although he was thought wise by many, and still wiser by himself; and thereupon I tried to explain to him that he thought himself wise, but was not really wise, and the consequence was that he hated me, and his enmity was shared by several who were present and heard me. So I left him, saying to myself, as I went away: Well, although I do not suppose that either of us knows anything really beautiful and good, I am better off than he is, --for he knows nothing, and thinks that he knows; I neither know nor think that I know.

VOICES
(From the audience)

Listen to the old sophist....He's tricking us...He's a know-it-all who says he knows nothing....

SOCRATES

Please! Let me speak. **(Pause)** Then I went to one man after another, being not unconscious of the enmity which I provoked, and I lamented and feared this. And I swear to you, Athenians, by the dog I swear! --for I must tell you the truth--the result of my mission was just this: I found that the men most in repute were all but the most foolish; and that others less esteemed were really wiser and better. After the politicians, I went to the poets; tragic, dithyrambic, and all sorts. Accordingly I took them some of the most elaborate passages in their own writings, and asked what was the meaning of them--thinking that they would teach me something. Will you believe me? I am almost ashamed to confess the truth, but I must say that there is hardly a person present who would not have talked better about their poetry than they did themselves. Then I knew that not by wisdom do poets write poetry, but by a sort of genius and inspiration; they are like diviners or soothsayers who also say many fine things, but do not understand the meaning of them.

VOICES
(From the audience)
Defend yourself, Meletus!....Listen to what he's saying about poets....

SOCRATES
(Holds up his hand to ward off the voices)
This inquisition has led to my having many enemies of the worst and most dangerous kind, and has given occasion also to many calumnies. And I am called wise, for my hearers always imagine that I myself possess the wisdom which I find wanting in others; but the truth is, O men of Athens, that God only is wise; and by his answer he intends to show that the wisdom of men is worth little or nothing; he is not speaking of Socrates, he is only using my name by way of illustration, as if he said, He, O men, is the wisest, who, like Socrates, knows that his wisdom is in truth worth nothing. And so I go about the world, obedient to the god, and search and make enquiry into the wisdom of any one, whether citizen or stranger, who appears to be wise; and my occupation quite absorbs me, and I have no time to give either to any public matter of interest or to any concern of my own, but I am in utter poverty by reason of my devotion to the god.

There is another thing--young men of the richer classes, who have not much to do, come about me of their own accord; they like to hear the pretenders examined, and they often imitate me, and proceed to examine others; there are plenty of persons, as they quickly discover, who think that they know something, but really know little or nothing; and then those who are examined by them instead of being angry with themselves are angry with me: This confounded Socrates, they say; this villainous misleader of youth! --and then if somebody asks them, Why, what evil does he practice or teach? They do not know, and cannot tell.

And this is the reason why my three accusers, Meletus and Anytus and Lycon, have set upon me; Meletus, who has a quarrel with me on behalf of the poets; Anytus, on behalf of the craftsmen and politicians; Lycon, on behalf of the rhetoricians: and, as I said at the beginning, I cannot expect to get rid of such a mass of calumny all in a moment. And this, O men of Athens, is the truth and the whole truth.

I have said enough in my defence against the first class of my accusers; I turn to the second class. They are headed by Meletus, that good man and true lover of his country, as he calls himself. Against these, too, I must try to make a defence: --Let us recall their affidavit: it contains something of this kind: It says that Socrates is a doer of evil, who corrupts the youth; and who does not believe in the gods of the State, but has other new divinities of his own. Such is the charge.

Come hither, Meletus, and let me ask a question of you. You think a great deal about the improvement of youth?

(MELETUS has arisen and now stands center stage)

MELETUS
Yes, I do.

SOCRATES
Tell the judges, then, who is their improver.
(Pauses while MELETUS remains silent)
Observe, Meletus, that you are silent, and have nothing to say.
(Pauses again)
Speak up, friend, and tell us who their improver is.

MELETUS
The laws.

SOCRATES
But that, my good sir, is not my meaning. I want to know who the person is, who, in the first place, knows the laws.

MELETUS
The judges, Socrates, who are present in court.

SOCRATES
What, do you mean to say, Meletus, that they are able to instruct and improve youth?

MELETUS
Certainly they are.

SOCRATES
What, all of them, or some only and not others?

MELETUS

All of them.

SOCRATES

By the goddess Here, that is good news! There are plenty of improvers, then. And what do you say of the audience, --do they improve them?

MELETUS

Yes, they do.

SOCRATES

And the senators?

MELETUS

Yes, the senators improve them.

SOCRATES

But perhaps the members of the assembly corrupt them? --or do they improve them?

MELETUS

They improve them.

SOCRATES

Then every Athenian improves and elevates them; all with the exception of myself; and I alone am their corruptor? Is that what you affirm?

MELETUS

That is what I stoutly affirm.

SOCRATES

I am very unfortunate if you are right. Happy indeed would be the condition of youth if they had one corrupter only, and all the rest of the world were their improvers.

And now, Meletus, I will ask you another question--by Zeus I will. Which is better, to live among bad citizens, or among good ones? Answer, friend, I say; the question is one which may be easily answered. Do not the good do their neighbours good, and the bad do them evil?

MELETUS

Certainly.

SOCRATES

And is there any one who would rather be injured than benefitted by those who live with him? Answer, my good friend, the law requires you to answer--does any one like to be injured?

MELETUS

Certainly not.

SOCRATES

And when you accuse me of corrupting and deteriorating the youth, do you allege that I corrupt them intentionally or unintentionally?

MELETUS

Intentionally, I say.

SOCRATES

But you have just admitted that the good do their neighbours good, and the evil do them evil. Am I, at my age, in such darkness and ignorance as not to know that if a man with whom I have to live is corrupted by me, I am very likely to be harmed by him; and yet I corrupt him, and intentionally, too--so you say, although neither I nor any other human being is ever likely to be convinced by you. But either I do not corrupt them, or I corrupt them unintentionally; and on either view of the case you lie. If my offense is unintentional, the law has no cognizance of unintentional offenses: you ought to have taken me privately, and warned and admonished me; for if I had been better advised, I should have left off doing what I only did unintentionally-- no doubt I should.

But still I should like to know, Meletus, in what I am affirmed to corrupt the young. I suppose you mean, as I infer from your indictment, that I teach them not to acknowledge the gods which the State acknowledges, but some other new divinities or spiritual agencies in their stead.

MELETUS
Yes, that I say emphatically.

SOCRATES
Then, by the gods, Meletus, of whom we are speaking, tell me and the court, in somewhat plainer terms, what you mean! For I do not as yet understand whether you affirm that I teach other men to acknowledge some gods, and therefore that I do believe in gods, and am not an entire atheist, or, do you mean that I am an atheist simply, and a teacher of atheism?

MELETUS
I mean the latter--that you are a complete atheist.

SOCRATES

What an extraordinary statement! Why do you think so, Meletus? Do you mean that I do not believe in the godhead of the sun or moon, like other men?

MELETUS

I assure you, judges, that he does not: for he says that the sun is stone, and the moon earth.

SOCRATES

Friend Meletus, you think that you are accusing Anaxagoras. Meletus, you really think that I do not believe in any god?

MELETUS

I swear by Zeus that you believe absolutely in none at all.

SOCRATES

Nobody will believe you, Meletus, and I am pretty sure that you do not believe yourself. I cannot help thinking, men of Athens, that Meletus is reckless and impudent, and that he has written this indictment in a spirit of mere wantonness and youthful bravado. Has he not compounded a riddle, thinking to try me?

I should like you, O men of Athens, to join me in examining what I conceive to be his inconsistency; and do you, Meletus, answer.

VOICES

(From the audience)

Don't answer, Meletus....He's trying to trick you, Meletus....Don't let him make a fool of you, Meletus....Keep still, Meletus.

SOCRATES

And I must remind the audience of my request that they would not make a disturbance if I speak in my accustomed manner: Did ever man, Meletus, believe in the existence of human things, and not of human beings?

VOICES

(From the audience)

We've heard enough from you, Socrates....Keep still, Meletus....Don't let him make a fool of you, Meletus.

SOCRATES

I wish, men of Athens, that he would answer, and not be always trying to get up an interruption. No, my friend; I will answer to you and to the court, as you refuse to answer for yourself. There is no man who ever did. But now please to answer the next question: Can a man believe in spiritual and divine agencies, and not in spirits or demigods?

BASILEUS

Meletus will reply.

MELETUS

He cannot.

SOCRATES

How lucky I am to have extracted that answer, by the assistance of the court! But then you swear in the indictment that I teach and believe in divine or spiritual agencies (new or old, no matter for that); at any rate, I believe in spiritual agencies--so you say and swear in the affidavit; and yet if I believe in divine beings, how can I help believing in spirits or demigods--must I not? Now

what are spirits or demigods? Are they not either gods or
the sons of gods?

MELETUS

Certainly they are.

SOCRATES

But this is what I call the facetious riddle invented by
you: the demigods or spirits are gods, and you say first
that I do not believe in gods, and then again that I do
believe in gods; that is, if I believe in demigods.
**(Turns away from MELETUS and addresses the
Jurors in the audience. MELETUS takes his seat)**
I have said enough in answer to the charge of Meletus: any
elaborate defence is unnecessary; but I know only too well
how many are the enmities which I have incurred, and this
is what will be my destruction if I am destroyed;--not
Meletus, nor yet Anytus, but the envy and detraction of the
world, which has been the death of many good men, and
will probably be the death of many more; there is no danger
of my being the last of them.

Some one will say: And are you not ashamed, Socrates, of
a course of life which is likely to bring you to an untimely
end? To him I may fairly answer: There you are mistaken:
a man who is good for anything ought not to calculate the
chance of living or dying; he ought only to consider
whether in doing anything he is doing right or wrong--
acting the part of a good man or of a bad.

Strange, indeed, would be my conduct, O men of Athens,
if I, who, when I was ordered by the generals at Potidaea
and Amphipolis and Delium, remained where they placed
me, like any other man, facing death--if now, when, as I

conceive and imagine, God orders me to fulfil the philosopher's mission of searching into myself and other men, I were to desert my post through fear of death, or any other fear; that would indeed be strange, and I might justly be arraigned in court for denying the existence of the gods, if I disobeyed the oracle because I was afraid of death, fancying that I was wise when I was not wise. And in this respect only I believe myself to differ from men in general, and may perhaps claim to be wiser than they are: --that whereas I know but little of the world below, I do not suppose that I know: but I do know that injustice and disobedience to a better, whether God or man, is evil and dishonourable, and I will never fear or avoid a possible good rather than a certain evil.

If you say to me, Socrates, this time we will not mind Anytus, and you shall be let off, but upon one condition, that you are not to enquire and speculate in this way any more, and that if you are caught doing so again you shall die; --if this was the condition on which you let me go, I should reply: Men of Athens, I honour and love you; but I shall obey God rather than you, and while I have life and strength I shall never cease from the practice and teaching of philosophy, exhorting any one whom I meet and saying to him after my manner: You, my friend, -- a citizen of the great and mighty and wise city of Athens, --are you not ashamed of heaping up the greatest amount of money and honour and reputation, and caring so little about wisdom and truth and the greatest improvement of the soul, which you never regard or heed at all? And I shall repeat the same words to every one whom I meet, young and old, citizen and alien, but especially to the citizens, inasmuch as they are my brethren. For know that this is the command of God; and I believe that no greater good has ever happened in the State than my service to the God. I tell you that virtue is not given by money, but that from virtue comes money and every other good of man, public as well as private. This is my teaching, and if this is the doctrine which corrupts the youth, I am a mischievous person. But if any one says that this is not my teaching, he is speaking an untruth. Wherefore, O men of Athens, I say to you, do as Anytus bids or not as Anytus bids, and either acquit me or not; but whichever you do, understand that I shall never alter my ways, not even if I have to die many times.

VOICES
(From the audience)
Shut up, old fool!.... He calls what he does a service to the State!....Listen to the old fool play the hero!....Shut him up!....What God is this he serves?

SOCRATES
Men of Athens, do not interrupt, but hear me; there was an understanding between us that you should hear me to the end. I would have you know, that if you kill such an one as I am, you will injure yourselves more than you will injure me. Nothing will injure me, not Meletus nor yet Anytus--for a bad man is not permitted to injure a better than himself.

And now, Athenians, I am not going to argue for my own sake, as you may think, but for yours, that you may not sin against the God by condemning me, who am his gift to you. For if you kill me you will not easily find a successor to me, who, if I may use such a ludicrous figure of speech, am a sort of gadfly, given to the State by God; and the State is a great and noble steed who is tardy in his motions owing to his very size, and requires to be stirred into life. I am that gadfly which God has attached to the State, and all day long and in all places am always fastening upon you, arousing and persuading and reproaching you. You will not easily find another like me, and therefore I would advise you to spare me. As you will perceive, not even the impudence of my accusers dares to say that I have ever exacted or sought pay of any one; of that they have no witness. And I have a sufficient witness to the truth of what I say--my poverty.

Some one may wonder why I go about in private giving advice and busying myself with the concerns of others, but do not venture to come forward in public and advise the State. I will tell you why. You have heard me speak at sundry times and in diverse places of an oracle or sign which comes to me, and is the divinity which Meletus ridicules in the indictment. This sign, which is a kind of voice, first began to come to me when I was a child; it always forbids but never commands me to do anything which I am going to do. This is what deters me from being a politician. And rightly, as I think. For I am certain, O men of Athens, that if I had engaged in politics, I should have perished long ago, and done no good either to you or to myself. For the truth is, that no man who goes to war with you or any other multitude, honestly striving against the many lawless and unrighteous deeds which are done in a State, will save his life.

I can give you convincing evidence of what I say, not words only, but what you value far more--actions. Let me relate to you a passage of my own life which will prove to you that I should never have yielded to injustice from any fear of death and that "as I should have refused to yield" I must have died at once. I will tell you a tale of the courts, not very interesting perhaps, but nevertheless true. The only office of State which I ever held, O men of Athens, was that of senator: the tribe Antiochis, which is my tribe, had the presidency at the trial of the generals who had not taken up the bodies of the slain after the battle of Arginusae; and you proposed to try them in a body, contrary to law, as you all thought afterwards; but at the time I was the only one of the Prytanes who was opposed to the illegality, and I gave my vote against you; and when the orators threatened to impeach and arrest me, and you called and shouted, I made up my mind that I would run the risk, having law and justice with me, rather than take part in your injustice because I feared imprisonment and death. This happened in the days of the democracy. But when the oligarchy of the Thirty was in power, they sent for me and four others into the rotunda, and bade us bring Leon the Salaminian from Salamis, as they wanted to put him to death. This was a specimen of the sort of commands which they were always giving with the view of implicating as many as possible in their crimes; and then I showed, not in word only but in deed, that, if I may be allowed to use such an expression, I cared not a straw for death, and that my great and only care was lest I should do an unrighteous or unholy thing. For the strong arm of that oppressive power did not frighten me into doing wrong; and when we came out of the rotunda the other four went to Salamis and fetched Leon, but I went quietly home. For which I might have lost my life, had not the power of the Thirty shortly afterwards come to an end. And many will witness to my words.

Do you really imagine that I could have survived all these years, if I had led a public life, supposing that like a good man I had always maintained the right and had made justice, as I ought, the first thing? No, indeed, men of Athens, neither I nor any other man. But if any one likes to come and hear me while I am pursuing my mission, whether he be young or old, he is not excluded. Nor do I converse only with those who pay; but any one, whether he be rich or poor, may ask and answer me and listen to my words; and whether he turns out to be a bad man or a good one, neither result can be justly imputed to me; for I never taught or professed to teach him anything. And if any one says that he has ever learned or heard anything from me in private which all the world has not heard, let me tell you that he is lying.

VOICES
(From the audience)
He taught Critias to be a tyrant!...And what of Alcibiades?...And Charmides?...He ran a school for tyrants!

SOCRATES
Men of Athens! I beg you. Let me finish. **(Pause)** But I shall be asked, Why do people delight in continually conversing with you? I have told you already, Athenians, the whole truth about this matter: they like to hear the cross-examination of the pretenders to wisdom; there is amusement in it. If I am or have been corrupting the youth, those of them who are now grown up and have become sensible that I gave them bad advice in the days of their youth should come forward as accusers, and take their revenge; or if they do not like to come themselves, some of their relatives, fathers, brothers, or other kinsmen, should say what evil their families have suffered at my hands. Now is their time. Many of them I see in the court. There is Crito, who is of the same age and of the same deme with myself, and there is Critobulus his

son, whom I also see. Then again there is Lysanias the
father of Aeschines--he is present; and also there is
Antiphon the father of Epigenes; and there are the brothers
of several who have associated with me. There is
Nicostratus the brother of Theodotus (now Theodotus
himself is dead, and therefore he, at any rate, will not seek
to stop him); and there is Paralus the son of Demodocus,
who had a brother Theages; and Adeimantus the son of
Ariston, whose brother Plato is present; and Aeantodorus,
who is the brother of Apollodorus, whom I also see. I
might mention a great many others, some of whom Meletus
should have produced as witnesses in the course of his
speech.

**(As he mentions these names, SOCRATES points to
those sitting on the stage with him and to his other
friends in the audience)**

Why should they support me with their testimony? Why,
indeed, except for the sake of truth and justice, and because
they know that I am speaking the truth, and that Meletus is
a liar.

Well, Athenians, this and the like of this is all the defence
which I have to offer. Yet a word more. Perhaps there
may be some one who is offended at me, when he calls to
mind how he himself on a similar, or even a less serious
occasion, prayed and entreated the judges with many tears,
and how he produced his children in court, which was a
moving spectacle, together with a host of relations and
friends; whereas I, who am probably in danger of my life,
will do none of these things. To him I may fairly reply:
My friend, I am a man, and like other men, a creature of
flesh and blood, and not "of wood or stone," as Homer
says; and I have a family, yes, and sons, O Athenians, three
in number, one almost a man, and two others who are still

young; and yet I will not bring any of them hither in order to petition you for an acquittal. And why not? Not from any self-assertion or want of respect for you. Whether I am or am not afraid of death is another question, of which I will not now speak. But, having regard to public opinion, I feel that such conduct would be discreditable to myself, and to you, and to the whole State. One who has reached my years, and who has a name for wisdom, ought not to demean himself.

But, setting aside the question of public opinion, there seems to be something wrong in asking a favour of a judge, and thus procuring an acquittal, instead of informing and convincing him. For his duty is, not to make a present of justice, but to give judgement. Do not then require me to do what I consider dishonourable and impious and wrong, especially now, when I am being tried for impiety on the indictment of Meletus. For if, O men of Athens, by force of persuasion and entreaty I could overpower your oaths, then I should be teaching you to believe that there are no gods, and in defending should simply convict myself of the charge of not believing in them. But that is not so--far otherwise. For I do believe that there are gods, and in a sense higher than that in which any of my accusers believe in them. And to you and to God I commit my cause, to be determined by you as is best for you and me.

(As the CHORUS begins, SOCRATES walks off LEFT)

CHORUS

You've heard him as he tried to trick Meletus
Into confusion as he did with Euthyphro
On his way to his own trial.
He boasts of his tremendous bravery

In war and peace. Those here who did not die
At Delium and Potidaea
Were also brave. He tells us he alone
Refused to try the Arginusae generals
In a group in the Old Democracy.
But what is right within democracy
Except the people's will?
There is no greater right than this.
And then he says he disobeyed the Thirty
When ordered to bring Leon from Salamis
To die. But we recall the man who was
Most powerful among the Thirty--
Socrates' disciple, his friend Critias!
What courage was it to defy his friend?
He calls his way of life a service to
The State--a gadfly we can do without.
He is God's gift to us, he says, and does
God's will. What God we ask--
That is the reason for this trial.
What God is this whom he proclaims to serve?
Not Zeus nor others that we know,
But a new and strange divinity,
Which speaks to him alone, but not to us.
It has a Voice. Whose Voice we ask
--The God's? or his?

ACT I

Scene 2

AT RISE: Lapse of time of 20-30 minutes while the vote is taken on Socrates' guilt. SOCRATES stands near center, with his friends seated at LEFT and his accusers at RIGHT. BASILEUS and the MAGISTRATES sit at back. At LEFT is a poster with the voting results of the JURY:

Guilty   280
Not Guilty   220

SOCRATES

There are many reasons why I am not grieved, O men of
Athens, at the vote of condemnation. I expected it, and
am only surprised that the votes are so nearly equal; for I
had thought that the majority against me would have been
far larger; but now, had thirty votes gone over to the
other side, I should have been acquitted.

And so Meletus proposes death as the penalty. And what
shall I propose on my part, O men of Athens? Clearly
that which is my due. And what is my due? What
returns shall be made to the man who has never had the
wit to be idle during his whole life? Reflecting that I
was really too honest a man to be a politician and live, I
did not go where I could do no good to you or to myself;
but where I could do the greatest good privately to every
one of you, thither I went, and sought to persuade every
man among you that he must look to himself, and seek
virtue and wisdom before he looks to his private interests;
and that this should be the order which he observes in all
his actions.   What shall be done to such an one?
Doubtless some good thing, O men of Athens, if he has
his reward. What would be a reward suitable to a poor
man who is your benefactor, and who desires leisure that
he may instruct you? There can be no reward so fitting
as maintenance in the Prytaneum, O men of Athens, a
reward which he deserves far more than the citizen who
has won the prize at Olympia in the horse or chariot race.
For I am in want, and he has enough; and he only gives
you the appearance of happiness, and I give you the
reality.

VOICES

(From the audience)

Ha, ha....Ha, ha....Listen to him....Ha, ha!

SOCRATES

I am convinced that I never intentionally wronged any one, although I cannot convince you--the time has been too short; if there were a law at Athens, as there is in other cities, that a capital cause should not be decided in one day, then I believe that I should have convinced you. But I cannot in a moment refute great slanders. I will not say of myself that I deserve any evil, or propose any penalty. Why should I? Because I am afraid of the penalty of death which Meletus proposes? I do not know whether death is a good or an evil. Shall I propose imprisonment? And why should I live in prison, and be the slave of the magistrate of the year--of the Eleven? Or shall the penalty be a fine, and imprisonment until the fine is paid? There is the same objection. I should have to lie in prison, for money I have none, and cannot pay. And if I say exile (and this may possibly be the penalty which you will affix), I must indeed be blinded by the love of life, if I am so irrational as to expect that when you, who are my own citizens, cannot endure my discourses and words, others are likely to endure me. No, indeed, men of Athens, that is not very likely. And what a life should I lead, at my age, wandering from city to city, ever changing my place of exile, and always being driven out!

Some one will say: Yes, Socrates, but cannot you hold your tongue, and then you may go into a foreign city, and no one will interfere with you? If I tell you that to do as you say would be a disobedience to the God, and therefore that I cannot hold my tongue, you will not believe that I am serious; and if I say again that the unexamined life is not worth living, you are still less likely to believe me. Had I money I might have estimated the offence at what I was able to pay, and not have been much the worse. But I have none, and therefore I must ask you to proportion the fine to my means. Well, perhaps I could afford a mina, and therefore I propose that penalty.

(While SOCRATES has been speaking, his friends on stage, CRITO, PLATO, CRITOBULUS, and APOLLODORUS, have been conferring. PLATO stands and ap-proaches SOCRATES and speaks privately to him. As SOCRATES continues to speak, PLATO returns to his seat)

SOCRATES

Plato, Crito, Critobulus, and Apollodorus, my friends here, bid me say thirty minae, and they will be the sureties. Let thirty minae be the penalty; for which sum they will be ample security to you.

CHORUS

So what does Socrates propose we give
To him as reward for the life he's led?
Support him in the Prytaneum
And let him go about as he has all
Along! Meletus asks for death but he
Requests we honor him!
If he had had more time, he says, he could
Convince the jury of his innocence.
By the goddess Here, we rejoice that we
No longer have to listen to his piece.
Prison or exile do not fit his wishes.

In exile he could never change his ways;
To do so he would disobey his God
And quiet his most eloquent tongue.
And so he offers to pay out a fine
Of thirty minae which his friends contribute.
Let us see what the judges think of that.

(As the CHORUS is finishing, the two MAGISTRATES leave at LEFT. BASILEUS remains. A poster is placed over the previous poster saying:

PENALTY:
For Death   360
For 30 Minae 140

SOCRATES

Not much time will be gained, O Athenians, in return for the evil name which you will get from the detractors of the city, who will say that you killed Socrates, a wise man. If you had waited a little while, your desire would have been fulfilled in the course of nature. For I am far advanced in years, as you may perceive, and not far from death. I am speaking now not to all of you, but only to those who have condemned me to death. And I have another thing to say to them: You think that I was convicted because I had no words of the sort which would have procured my acquittal. But I had not the boldness or impudence or inclination to address you as you would have liked me to do, weeping and wailing and lamenting, and saying and doing many things which you have been accustomed to hear from others, and which, as I maintain, are unworthy of me. I would rather die having spoken after my manner, than speak in your manner and live. For neither in war nor yet at law ought I or any man to use every way of escaping death. The difficulty, my friends, is not to avoid death, but to avoid unrighteousness; for that runs faster than death.

And now, O men who have condemned me, I would fain prophesy to you; for I am about to die, and in the hour of death men are gifted with prophetic power. And I prophesy to you who are my murderers, that immediately after my departure punishment far heavier than you have inflicted on me will surely await you. Me you have killed because you wanted to escape the accuser, and not to give an account of your lives. If you think that by killing men you can prevent some one from censuring your evil lives, you are mistaken; that is not a way of escape which is either possible or honourable; the easiest and the noblest way is not to be disabling others, but to be improving yourselves. This is the prophecy which I utter before my departure to the judges who have condemned me.

(MELETUS, ANYTUS, and LYCON rise and walk noisily out. At this signal, some of Socrates' detractors in the audience leave, talking among themselves)

SOCRATES
Friends, who would have acquitted me, I would like also to talk with you about the thing which has come to pass, while the magistrates are busy, and before I go to the place at which I must die. Stay then a little, for we may as well talk with one another while there is time. You are my friends, and I should like to show you the meaning of this event which has happened to me. O my

judges--for you I may truly call judges--I should like to tell you of a wonderful circumstance. Hitherto the divine faculty has constantly been in the habit of opposing me even about trifles, if I was going to make a slip or error in any matter; and now as you see there has come upon me that which may be thought, and is generally believed to be, the last and worst evil. But the oracle made no sign of opposition, either when I was leaving my house in the morning, or when I was on my way to the court, or while I was speaking, at anything which I was going to say. What do I take to be the explanation of this silence? I will tell you. It is an intimation that what has happened to me is a good, and that those of us who think that death is an evil are in error.

Let us reflect and we shall see that there is great reason to hope that death is a good; for one of two things--either death is a state of nothingness and utter unconsciousness, or, as men say, there is a change and migration of the soul from this world to another. Now, if you suppose that there is no consciousness, but a sleep like the sleep of him who is undisturbed even by dreams, death will be an unspeakable gain. If death be of such a nature, I say that to die is gain; for eternity is then only a single night. But if death is the journey to another place, and there, as men say, all the dead abide, what good, O my friends and judges, can be greater than this? If, indeed, when the pilgrim arrives in the world below, he is delivered from the professors of justice in this world, and finds the true judges who are said to give judgement there, that pilgrimage will be worth making. What would not a man give if he might converse with Orpheus and Musaeus and Hesiod and Homer? Nay, if this be true, let me die again and again. I myself, too, shall have a wonderful interest in there meeting and conversing with Palamedes, and Ajax, and any other ancient hero who has suffered death through an unjust judgement. Above all, I shall then be able to continue my search into true and false knowledge; as in this world, so also in the next; and I shall find out who is wise, and who pretends to be wise, and is not. What would not a man give, O judges, to be able to examine the leader of the great Trojan expedition; or Odysseus or Sisyphus, or numberless others, men and women too! What infinite delight would there be in conversing with them and asking them questions! In another world they do not put a man to death for asking questions: assuredly not. For besides being happier than we are, they will be immortal, if what is said is true.

Wherefore, O judges, be of good cheer about death, and know of a certainty, that no evil can happen to a good man, either in life or after death. He and his are not neglected by the gods; nor has my own approaching end happened by mere chance. But I see clearly that the time had arrived when it was better for me to die and be released from trouble; wherefore the oracle gave no sign. For which reason, also, I am not angry with my condemners, or with my accusers; they have done me no harm, although they did not mean to do me any good; and for this I may gently blame them.

Still, I have a favour to ask of you, my friends. When my sons are grown up, I would ask you to punish them; and I would have you trouble them, as I have troubled you, if they seem to care abut riches, or anything, more than about virtue; or if they pretend to be something when they are really nothing,--then reprove them, as I have reproved you, for not caring about that for which they ought to care and thinking that they are something when they are really nothing. If you do this, both I and my sons will have received justice at your hands.

(ENTER JAILER who stands beside Socrates)

The hour of departure has arrived, and we go our ways--I to die, and you to live. Which is better God only knows.

(EXIT JAILER AND SOCRATES. As they go out, PLATO, CRITO, CRITOBULUS, and APOLLODORUS stand. EXIT BASILEUS)

CHORUS

Alas, we did not seek to kill him. Let
Him flee. That was Anytus' true intent,
Only that, that he would leave the city.
How did we know that he would choose to die
A martyr with blood spilled upon our hands?
Why did he speak before the jurors thus
Saying he is the wisest of all men,
Politicians are merely fools, and poets
Have inspiration but no wisdom?
A court must be a place of dignity;
One ought to be respectful there, though one
Be innocent, as Socrates. Why did
He treat Meletus so and anger him?
Socrates forgot he spoke not to Meletus
In the marketplace.
Was he too proud to beg for mercy when
His life was being threatened? If he
Had done so, we would fain have spared him.

He says it is a God divine who guides him.
What is it we have done today?

CURTAIN

CRITO

Cast of characters

CRITO: A wealthy Athenian of the same age as Socrates and a friend. He pleads with Socrates to escape, his chief reason being the disgrace which Socrates' friends will suffer because it will appear that Crito and Socrates' other friends "lacked either the influence or the will to rescue their master." (Paul Shorey, *What Plato Said*) According to R. E. Allen in *Socrates and Legal Obligation*, "Crito's preoccupation with shame and disgrace is not to be dismissed as accidental or idiosyncratic." Rather, concern for appearance was a chief factor of traditional Greek morality at that time.

SOCRATES: A citizen of Athens, 70 years old, sentenced to die. Socrates has been found "guilty of refusing to recognize the gods recognized by the state, and of introducing other new divinities. He is also guilty of corrupting the youth." (Diogenes Laertius, quoted by R. E. Allen) R. E. Allen says,

> He was tried the day after the priest of Apollo crowned the stern of the sacred ship which Athens sent each year to Delos, Apollo's major shrine, in thanksgiving to the God. While the ship was gone, the City was kept ritually clean, and no executions were performed .....On this occasion the ship was detained by contrary winds, and Socrates had to endure a fairly lengthy imprisonment.

Although in the *Apology* Socrates told of two instances in which he had refused to obey orders of government because he regarded the orders as unjust or unholy, in the matter of escape he insists upon obeying the law. There is no contradiction in Socrates' decisions, however, as R. E. Allen explains. One may refuse to obey the law if the law requests one to *do* something unjust or unholy, but when the law orders one to *suffer* injustice, one must obey it. To refuse to obey the law in order not to *suffer* injustice is, as Socrates argues here, a violation of law and order in the state. Richard Kraut explains the decision of Socrates not to escape thus:

> Socrates was clearheaded enough to see that you cannot be unconditionally committed both to justice and obedience. He insists that when an order calls upon a citizen to act in a way that conflicts with virtue, he must refuse. (*Socrates and the State*)

CHORUS: Two or more Athenians. The tone of the Chorus has changed from that of the *Apology*, in which the Chorus reflected the mood of the jurors, who behaved somewhat like a mob, and the atmosphere, R. E. Allen says, was "very like a circus." Here the Chorus recognizes the gravity of the action of the court.

SCENE: The prison in Athens.

TIME: 399 B.C. Shortly before dawn.

SETTING: A room in the prison in Athens where Socrates has been confined since his trial. A bench and a simple bed resembling a cot are the only furniture. A door and a window are at back, near center.

AT RISE: It is before dawn. CRITO is seen sitting quietly on the bench. SOCRATES is asleep on the bed. As the action proceeds, the light becomes brighter, as seen through the door and the window. Each of Socrates' legs has a chain on them. The chain extends between the legs, giving him an opportunity to make moderate steps. An extension of the chain leads to the door and beyond.

CHORUS
We wait for the day when we may forget
This thing that we have done.

Obediently, our prisoner expects
His fate. The wait's been long for him and for
Us too. Why have his friends not aided him
To flee our city while the jailer looked
The other way? To Thebes or to Megara
He could go, perhaps, to Thessaly
Where Socrates' friend Crito has great influence.
If he would go, we could forget the day
--That awful day we sentenced him to die.
He would not stand and weep before us at
His trial, beseeching us for our good mercy.
We only did what we thought we must do.

The ship from Delium approaches Athens.
When it arrives, no longer then the city
Retains its ritual cleanliness, no more
Delays the ministration of his death.
Go, Socrates, flee now before the hour
Of your demise has come.

(As the CHORUS is finishing, SOCRATES awakes, sits up, puts his feet on the floor, and notices CRITO)

SOCRATES

Why have you come at this hour, Crito? It must be quite early?

CRITO

(Rising)
Yes, certainly.

SOCRATES

What is the exact time?

CRITO
(Walking to the door)
The dawn is breaking.

SOCRATES
I wonder that the keeper of the prison would let you in.

CRITO
(Turning back to Socrates)
He knows me, because I often come, Socrates; moreover, I have done him a kindness.

SOCRATES
And are you only just arrived?

CRITO
No, I came some time ago.

SOCRATES
Then why did you sit and say nothing, instead of at once awakening me?

CRITO
(Sitting again on the bench)
I have been watching with amazement your peaceful slumbers; and for that reason I did not awake you, because I wished to minimize the pain. I have always thought you to be of a happy disposition; but never did I see anything like the easy, tranquil manner in which you bear this calamity.

SOCRATES
Why, Crito, when a man has reached my age he ought not to be repining at the approach of death.

CRITO

And yet other old men find themselves in similar misfortunes, and age does not prevent them from repining.

SOCRATES

That is true. But you have not told me why you come at this early hour.

CRITO

I come to bring you a message which is sad and painful; not, as I believe, to yourself, but to all of us who are your friends, and saddest of all to me.

SOCRATES

What? Has the ship come from Delos, on the arrival of which I am to die?

CRITO

No, the ship has not actually arrived, but she will probably be here to-day, as persons who have come from Sunium tell me that they left her there; and therefore tomorrow, Socrates, will be the last day of your life.

SOCRATES

Very well, Crito; if such is the will of God, I am willing; but my belief is that there will be a delay of a day.

CRITO

Why do you think so?

SOCRATES

I will tell you. I am to die on the day after the arrival of the ship.

CRITO
Yes; that is what the authorities say.

SOCRATES
But I do not think that the ship will be here until to-morrow; this I infer from a vision which I had last night, or rather only just now, when you fortunately allowed me to sleep.

CRITO
And what was the nature of the vision?

SOCRATES
There appeared to me the likeness of a woman, fair and comely, clothed in bright raiment, who called to me and said,

"O Socrates,

"The third day hence to fertile Phthia shalt thou go."

CRITO
What a singular dream, Socrates!

SOCRATES
There can be no doubt about the meaning, Crito, I think.

CRITO
Yes; the meaning is only too clear. But, oh! my beloved Socrates, let me entreat you once more to take my advice and escape. For if you die I shall not only lose a friend who can never be replaced, but there is another evil: people who do not know you and me will believe that I might have saved you if I had been willing to give money, but that I did not care.

SOCRATES

But why, my dear Crito, should we care about the opinion of the many? Good men, and they are the only persons who are worth considering, will think of these things truly as they occurred.

CRITO

But you see, Socrates, that the opinion of the many must be regarded, for what is now happening shows that they can do the greatest evil to anyone who has lost their good opinion.

SOCRATES

I only wish it were so, Crito; and that the many could do the greatest evil; for then they would also be able to do the greatest good--and what a fine thing this would be! But in reality they can do neither; for they cannot make a man either wise or foolish; and whatever they do is the result of chance.

CRITO

Well, I will not dispute with you; but please to tell me, Socrates, whether you are not acting out of regard to me and your other friends: are you not afraid that if you escape from prison we may get into trouble with the informers for having stolen you away, and lose either the whole or a great part of our property; or that even a worse evil may happen to us? Now, if you fear on our account, be at ease; for in order to save you, we ought surely to run this, or even a greater risk; be persuaded, then, and do as I say.

SOCRATES

Yes, Crito, that is one fear which you mention, but by no means the only one.

CRITO
(Rises and walks back and forth as he speaks)

Fear not--there are persons who are willing to get you out of prison at no great cost; and as for the informers, they are far from being exorbitant in their demands--a little money will satisfy them. My means, which are certainly ample, are at your service, and if you have a scruple about spending all mine, here are strangers who will give you the use of theirs; and one of them, Simmias the Theban, has brought a large sum of money for this very purpose; and Cebes and many others are prepared to spend their money in helping you to escape. I say, therefore, do not hesitate on our account, and do not say, as you did in the court, that you will have a difficulty in knowing what to do with yourself anywhere else. For men will love you in other places to which you may go, and not in Athens only; there are friends of mine in Thessaly, if you like to go to them, who will value and protect you, and no Thessalian will give you any trouble. Nor can I think that you are at all justified, Socrates, in betraying your own life when you might be saved; in acting thus you are playing into the hands of your enemies, who are hurrying on your destruction. And further I should say that you are deserting your own children. No man should bring children into the world who is unwilling to persevere to the end in their nurture and education. The trial need never have come on, or might have been managed differently; and this last act, or crowning folly, will seem to have occurred through our negligence and cowardice, who might have saved you, if we had been good for anything. Make up your mind, then, or rather have your mind already made up, for the time of deliberation is over, and there is only one thing to be done, which must be done this very night, and if we delay at all will be no longer practicable or possible; I beseech you, Socrates, be persuaded by me, and do as I say.

SOCRATES

Dear Crito, your zeal is invaluable, if a right one; but if wrong, the greater the zeal the greater the danger; and therefore we ought to consider whether I shall or shall not do as you say. I cannot repudiate my own words: the principles which I have hitherto honoured and revered I still honour, and unless we can at once find other and better principles, I am certain not to agree with you. What will be the fairest way of considering the question? Shall I return to your old argument about the opinions of men?--we were saying that some of them are to be regarded, and others not. That argument, which, as I believe is maintained by many persons of authority, was to the effect, as I was saying, that the opinions of some men are to be regarded, and of other men not to be regarded. Now you, Crito, are not going to die to-morrow--at least, there is no human probability of this--and therefore you are disinterested and not liable to be deceived by the circumstances in which you are placed. Tell me whether I am right in saying that some opinions, and the opinions of some men only, are to be valued, and that other opinions, and the opinions of other men, are not to be valued. I ask you whether I was right in maintaining this?

CRITO
(Sitting down on the bench)
Certainly.

SOCRATES

The good are to be regarded, and not the bad?

CRITO

Yes.

SOCRATES

And the opinions of the wise are good, and the opinions of the unwise are evil?

CRITO

Certainly.

SOCRATES

And what was said about another matter? Is the pupil who devotes himself to the practice of gymnastics supposed to attend to the praise and blame and opinion of every man, or of one man only--his physician or trainer, whoever he may be?

CRITO

Of one man only.

SOCRATES

And if he disobeys and disregards the opinion and approval of the one, and regards the opinion of the many who have no understanding, will he not suffer?

CRITO

Certainly he will.

SOCRATES

And what will the evil be in the disobedient person?

CRITO

Clearly, affecting the body; that is what is destroyed by the evil.

SOCRATES

(Rises, walks back and forth, sometimes stopping in front of Crito)

Very good; and is not this true, Crito, of other things which we need not separately enumerate? In questions of just and unjust, fair and foul, good and evil, which are the subjects of our present consultation, ought we to follow the opinion of the many and to fear them; or the opinion of the one man who has understanding? Ought we not to fear and reverence him more than all the rest of the world: and if we desert him shall we not destroy and injure that principle in us which may be assumed to be improved by justice and deteriorated by injustice--there is such a principle?

CRITO

Certainly there is, Socrates.

SOCRATES

And will life be worth having, if that higher part of man be destroyed, which is improved by justice and depraved by injustice? Do we suppose that principle, whatever it may be in man, which has to do with justice and injustice, to be inferior to the body?

CRITO

Certainly not.

SOCRATES

More honourable than the body?

CRITO
Far more.

SOCRATES
Then, my friend, we must not regard what the many say of us; but what he, the one man who has understanding of just and unjust, will say, and what the truth will say. And therefore you begin in error when you advise that we should regard the opinion of the many about just and unjust, good and evil, honourable and dishonourable-- "Well," some one will say, "but the many can kill us."

CRITO
Yes, Socrates; that will clearly be the answer.

SOCRATES
And it is true: but still I find with surprise that the old argument is unshaken as ever. And I should like to know whether I may say the same of another proposition--that not life, but a good life, is to be chiefly valued?

CRITO
Yes, that also remains unshaken.

SOCRATES
And a good life is equivalent to a just and honourable one--that holds also?

CRITO
Yes, it does.

SOCRATES
From these premisses I proceed to argue the question whether I ought or ought not to try to escape without the

consent of the Athenians; and if I am clearly right in escaping, then I will make the attempt; but if not, I will abstain. Let us consider the matter together, and do you either refute me if you can, and I will be convinced; or else cease, my dear friend, from repeating to me that I ought to escape against the wishes of the Athenians. And now please to consider my first position, and try how you can best answer me.

CRITO

I will.

SOCRATES

Are we to say that we are never intentionally to do wrong, or that in one way we ought and in another way we ought not to do wrong, or is doing wrong always evil and dishonourable, as I was just now saying, and as has been already acknowledged by us? Shall we say so or not?

CRITO

Yes.

SOCRATES

Then we must do no wrong?

CRITO

Certainly not.

SOCRATES

Nor when injured injure in return, as the many imagine; for we must injure no one at all?

CRITO

Clearly not.

SOCRATES

Again, Crito, may we do evil?

CRITO

Surely not, Socrates.

SOCRATES

And what of doing evil in return for evil, which is the morality of the many--is that just or not?

CRITO

Not just.

SOCRATES

For doing evil to another is the same as injuring him?

CRITO

Very true.

SOCRATES

Then we ought not to retaliate or render evil for evil to any one, whatever evil we may have suffered from him. But I would have you consider, Crito, whether you really mean what you are saying. For this opinion has never been held, and never will be held, by any considerable number of persons; and those who are agreed and those who are not agreed upon this point have no common ground, and can only despise one another when they see how widely they differ. Tell me, then, whether you agree with my first principle, that neither injury nor retaliation nor warding off evil by evil is ever right. And shall that be the premiss of our argument?

CRITO
You may proceed, for I have not changed my mind.

SOCRATES
Then I will go on to the next point, which may be put in the form of a question: --Ought a man to do what he admits to be right, or ought he to betray the right?

CRITO
He ought to do what he thinks right.

SOCRATES
But if this is true, what is the application? In leaving the prison against the will of the Athenians, do I wrong any? or rather do I not wrong those whom I ought least to wrong? Do I not desert the principles which were acknowledged by us to be just--what do you say?

CRITO

I cannot tell, Socrates; for I do not know.

SOCRATES
Then consider the matter in this way: --Imagine that I am about to play truant (you may call the proceeding by any name which you like), and the laws and the government come and interrogate me: "Tell us, Socrates," they say; "what are you about? are you not going by an act of yours to overturn us--the laws, and the whole State, as far as in you lies? Do you imagine that a State can subsist and not be overthrown, in which the

decisions of law have no power, but are set aside and trampled upon by individuals?" What will be our answer, Crito, to these and the like words? Shall we reply, "Yes; but the State has injured us and given an unjust sentence." Suppose I say that?

CRITO

Very good, Socrates.

SOCRATES

"And was that our agreement with you?" the law would answer; "or were you to abide by the sentence of the State? What complaint have you to make against us which justifies you in attempting to destroy us and the State? In the first place, did we not bring you into existence? Your father married your mother by our aid and begat you. Say whether you have any objection to urge against those of us who regulate marriage?" None, I should reply. "Or against those of us who after birth regulate the nurture and education of children, in which you also were trained? Were not the laws, which have the charge of education, right in commanding your father to train you in music and gymnastic?" Right, I should reply. "Well, then, since you were brought into the world and nurtured and educated by us, can you deny in the first place that you are our child and slave, as your fathers were before you? And if this is true, you are not on equal terms with us; nor can you think that you have a right to do to us what we are doing to you. And because we think right to destroy you, do you think that you have any right to destroy us in return, and your country as far as in you lies? Will you, O professor of true virtue, pretend that you are justified in this? Has a philosopher like you failed to discover that our country is more to be valued and higher and holier far than mother or father or any ancestor, and more to be regarded in the eyes of the gods and of men of understanding? Whether in battle or in a court of law, or in any other place, the citizen must do what his city and his country order him; or he must change their view of what is just: and if he may do no violence to his father or mother, much less may he do violence to his country." What answer shall we make to this, Crito? Do the laws speak truly, or do they not?

CRITO
I think that they do.

SOCRATES
Then the laws will say: "Consider, Socrates, if we are speaking truly that in your present attempt you are going to do us an injury. For, having brought you into the world, and nurtured and educated you, and given you and every other citizen a share in every good which we had to give, we further proclaim to any Athenian by the liberty which we allow him, that if he does not like us when he has become of age and has seen the ways of the city, he may go where he pleases and take his goods with him. None of us laws will forbid him or interfere with him. Any one who does not like us and the city, and who wants to emigrate to a colony or to any other city, may go where he likes, retaining his property.

"Moreover, you might in the course of the trial, if you had liked, have fixed the penalty at banishment; the State which refuses to let you go now would have let you go then. But you pretended that you preferred death to exile, and that you were not unwilling to die. And, answer this question: Are we right in saying that you agreed to be governed according to us in deed, and not in word only? Is that true or not?" How shall we answer, Crito? Must we not assent?

CRITO
We cannot help it, Socrates.

SOCRATES
Then will they not say: "You, Socrates, are breaking the covenants and agreements which you made with us at your leisure, not in any haste or under any compulsion or deception, but after you have had seventy years to think of them, during which time you were at liberty to leave the city, if we were not to your mind, or if our covenants appeared to you to be unfair. Whereas you, above all other Athenians, seemed to be so fond of the State, or, in other words, of us, her laws (and who would care about a State which has no laws?), that you never stirred out of her.

"For just consider, if you transgress and err in this sort of way, what good will you do either to yourself or to your friends? That your friends will be driven into exile and deprived of citizenship, or will lose their property, is tolerably certain; and you yourself, if you fly to one of the neighbouring cities, as, for example, Thebes or Megara, both of which are well governed, will come to them as an enemy, Socrates, and their government will be against you, and all patriotic citizens will cast an evil eye upon you as a subverter of the laws, and you will confirm in the minds of the judges the justice of their own condemnation of you. For he who is a corrupter of the laws is more than likely to be a corrupter of the young and foolish portion of mankind. Will you then flee from well-ordered cities and virtuous men? and is existence worth having on these terms?

"If you go away from well-governed States to Crito's friends in Thessaly, where there is great disorder and license, they will be charmed to hear the tale of your escape from prison, set off with ludicrous particulars of the manner in which you were wrapped in a goatskin or some other disguise, and metamorphosed as the manner is of runaways; but will there be no one to remind you that in your old age you were not ashamed to violate the most sacred laws from a miserable desire of a little more life? Perhaps not, if you keep them in a good temper; but if they are out of temper you will hear many degrading things; you will live, but how? --as the flatterer of all men, and the servant of all men; and doing what? --eating and drinking in Thessaly, having gone abroad in order that you may get a dinner. And where will be your fine sentiments about justice and virtue? Say that you wish to live for the sake of your children--you want to bring them up and educate them--will you take them into Thessaly and deprive them of Athenian citizenship?

"Listen, then, Socrates, to us who have brought you up. Think not of life and children first, and of justice afterwards, but of justice first, that you may be justified before the princes of the world below. Now you depart in innocence, a sufferer and not a doer of evil; a victim, not of the laws but of men. But if you go forth, returning evil for evil, and injury for injury, breaking the covenants and agreements which you have made with us, and wronging those whom you ought least of all to wrong, that is to say, yourself, your friends, your country, and us, we shall be angry with you while you live, and our brethren, the laws in the world below, will receive you as an enemy; for they will know that you have done your best to destroy us. Listen, then, to us and not to Crito."

This, dear Crito, is the voice which I seem to hear murmuring in my ears, like the sound of the flute in the ears of the mystic; that voice is humming in my ears, and prevents me from hearing any other. And I know that anything more which you may say will be vain. Yet speak, if you have anything to say.

CRITO
(Rising)
I have nothing to say, Socrates.

SOCRATES
Leave me then, Crito, to fulfil the will of God, and to follow whither he leads.
(As the CHORUS begins, CRITO is seen slowly and sadly going out the door. As the CHORUS proceeds, SOCRATES walks to the window and is last seen in profile gazing toward the sky)

CHORUS
We should have known that he could not be tempted;
This Alcibiades told us long ago
At the house of Agathon. With bare feet
At Potidaea he trod upon the ice,
And did not suffer when there was no food.
As we fled from Delium he walked
Without fear and protected others.
"This is the sort of man who's never touched in war."
What is this covenant of which he speaks
Between the laws and citizens, which binds

Him to Athens when he's doomed to die?
We do not understand this man unlike
All others, brave in war, in peace proclaiming
Flight from a sentence, though unjust,
Would be to try to overturn the law.

Athens must have his life, he says, because
For seventy years he has enjoyed life here.
It is the will of God that it must be.

CURTAIN